# VIRTUAL HISTORY TOURS

## Look around a

# ROMAN AMPHITHEATER

## Jane Bingham

ARCTURUS

This edition first published by Arcturus Publishing
Distributed by Black Rabbit Books
123 South Broad Street
Mankato
Minnesota MN 56001

Printed in China

Library of Congress Cataloging-in-Publication Data
Bingham, Jane.
    Look around a Roman amphitheater / by Jane Bingham.
        p. cm. -- (Virtual history tours)
Includes index.
ISBN 978-1-84193-721-2 (alk. paper)
1. Amphitheaters--Rome--Juvenile literature.
2. Games--Rome--Juvenile literature. I. Title.

DG135.5.B56 2007
937--dc22
                        2007007561


9 8 7 6 5 4 3 2

Series concept: Alex Woolf
Editor: Jenni Rainford
Designer: Ian Winton
Plan artwork: Phil Gleaves

Picture credits:
Art Archive: 4 (Archaeological Museum Naples / Dagli Orti), 11 (Museo di Navarra Pamplona / Dagli Orti),
16 (Araldo de Luca), 18 (Bibliothèque des Artes Décoratifs Paris / Dagli Orti), 19 (Archaeological Museum
Madrid / Dagli Orti), 23 (Antioch Museum Turkey / Dagli Orti), 26 (Dagli Orti), 27 (Museo Nazionale
Reggio Calabria / Dagli Orti), 29 (Archaeological Museum Istanbul / Dagli Orti)
Corbis: 6 (Alinari Archives), 7 (Danny Lehman), 8 (Archivo Iconografico, S.A.), 9 (Charles and Josette Lenars),
10 (Stephanie Colasanti), 12 (Robert Holmes), 13 (Allinari Archives), 14 (Bettmann), 15 (Araldo de Luca),
17 (Araldo de Luca), 20 (Araldo de Luca), 22 (Gianni Dagli Orti), 24 (Bettmann), 25 (Christie's Images),
28 (Alinari Archives)
Arcturus Publishing Ltd: 21

# CONTENTS

Welcome to your tour of a Roman amphitheater! During your visit, you'll explore every part of the vast, circular stadium that the ancient Romans built for staging entertainments. You'll take a ringside seat beside the arena to see the day's events—but be warned, they will be bloodthirsty! You'll also see what happens beneath the stage, where you'll find animals, gladiators, and prisoners—all waiting to face the horrors of the arena.

## Roman Games

All over the Roman Empire, people flocked to amphitheaters to see violent shows, known as "the Games." The Games included wild animal hunts and even public executions, but the main events were the gladiator fights. Gladiators were trained warriors who fought each other to entertain the crowds. Their dramatic battles often ended in death.

## How the Games began

The first gladiator fights were performed as part of funerals. These solemn events acted out the battle triumphs of dead heroes. But gradually, the fights became very popular in their own right. By 100 BCE, special stadiums were being built so that large crowds could watch the Games. The first amphitheaters were made from wood, but by the second century CE, there were vast stone amphitheaters all over the Roman world.

Most gladiators wore body protection like this bronze helmet, which dates from the first century CE.

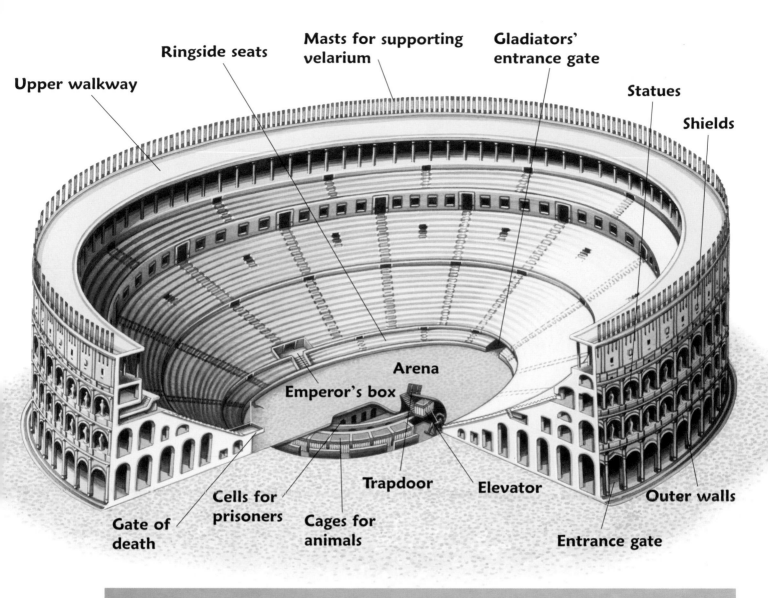

Upper walkway

Ringside seats

Masts for supporting velarium

Gladiators' entrance gate

Statues

Shields

Emperor's box

Arena

Trapdoor

Elevator

Outer walls

Gate of death

Cells for prisoners

Cages for animals

Entrance gate

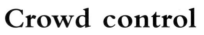

Your tour will take you to all the areas shown in this cutaway view of a Roman amphitheater.

In his record of his reign, Augustus, the first Roman emperor, listed some of the shows that he provided for his people:

*I gave a gladiatorial show three times in my own name and five times in the names of my sons or grandsons; at these shows about 10,000 fought.*

Augustus, *Deeds of the Divine Augustus*, first century CE

# Crowd control

The amphitheater you will explore is based on the Colosseum in Rome. This massive building was opened in 80 CE by a Roman emperor named Titus. It was the biggest stadium in the Roman world, and it could hold a crowd of 50,000 people.

# THE OUTER WALLS

**The outer walls**

Take a walk around the amphitheater's massive walls. They are built from travertine—a gleaming, pale gray stone dug from quarries near Rome. Inside their stone coating, the upper walls are built from brick and concrete. As you walk around, you'll see that the amphitheater has three levels of columns and arches, standing one on top of the other. The upper story has columns, but windows rather than arches.

## Using concrete

In the second century BCE, the Romans invented concrete. This new building material was light, strong, and easy to use. Roman builders mixed water with ash from volcanoes, then added small stones to give the mixture extra strength. Many Roman walls were built with two outer layers of brick filled with concrete, a bit like a sandwich. This method of building walls allowed the Romans to build very tall buildings that did not collapse under their own weight.

The Colosseum in Rome is amazingly strong. It has survived for 2,000 years.

6

# Using arches

By using columns and arches, the Romans were able to build much higher than ever before. Arches are surprisingly strong because each stone in the arch pushes hard against the stones on either side of it. This sideways pressure helps to hold the arch together. The spreading out of the pressure also makes the arches strong enough to support another set of columns and arches on top of them.

The Romans used arches to build structures that were light but also incredibly strong.

In Roman times, the Colosseum in Rome was known as Caesar's Amphitheater. The poet Martial wrote a poem listing all the best buildings in the world and ended with these lines:

*Let all works yield to Caesar's Amphitheater. Fame will speak of this one work in preference to any others.*

Martial, *Liber Spectaculorum*, first century CE

## Roman builders

In Roman times, building was very tough and dangerous work. Slaves did most of the jobs on a building site. Some worked as stonemasons, bricklayers, and carpenters, while others mixed concrete and carried heavy weights. Huge wooden cranes were used to lift stones and other heavy materials. Slaves operated the cranes by walking around and around inside a wheel that winched up the materials.

# STATUES AND SHIELDS

As you stroll around the amphitheater, you'll notice the rows of painted statues standing in archways. These form an impressive procession of gods and goddesses, ancient heroes, and outstanding emperors. Such splendid figures remind the Romans of their beliefs and the glorious history of their people. You'll also see the giant shields fixed to the walls of the upper story, glinting in the sunshine. These act as a reminder of the power of the Roman army.

**Shields**

**Statues**

## Power and glory

The massive amphitheaters at the heart of Roman cities were more than just great buildings. They were also symbols of Roman power and glory. Every time a crowd entered an amphitheater, they were filled with pride at being Roman. The Roman people were also reminded of the important things in their lives—religion, the empire, and the army.

Diana was the Roman goddess of hunting. Amphitheaters contained statues of her, and all the animal shows were dedicated to her.

# Roman religion

The Romans worshipped many different gods and goddesses and built temples and statues in honor of them. They also treated their emperors as gods. At the start of the Games, in front of the huge crowd, Roman priests held grand public ceremonies that included special prayers to the gods. Everyone in the empire had a duty to honor and worship the gods and the emperors. In fact, anyone who refused could be put to death in the arena!

In this passage, an anonymous writer explains that gladiator fights were an excellent way of preparing soldiers for battle:

*Romans about to go to war should have seen battle and wounds and steel, and naked men fighting against each other, that they might not fear armed men or shrink from blood or wounds.*

Historia Augusta,
fourth century CE

# Gladiators and soldiers

The Games were a great way of showing off the Romans' fighting skills. They reminded the Roman people of the power of their army. They also sent a clear message to any foreigners that the Romans were a force to be reckoned with. Roman emperors held special Games before a battle to fill their armies with fighting spirit and inspire soldiers to fight bravely.

GLADIATORS AND SOLDIERS: SEE PAGES 18-19

Like some gladiators, Roman soldiers used shields for protection. This battle formation is called the "tortoise."

9

# AN ENTRANCE GATE

Once you've seen the outside of the stadium, it's time to head inside, through one of the entrance gates. Just inside the gate, you'll see a wooden booth, which is where you collect your ticket to the Games. Tickets are made from bone and shaped like small coins. Each ticket is stamped with a different seat number, but choosing the right seat isn't easy!

**An entrance gate**

## Know your place!

The seating in a Roman amphitheater was strictly divided into five separate blocks, each for a different group in society. Ringside seats were closest to the arena. These were made from marble and were reserved for senators (members of the ruling class). Behind the senators sat the *equites*—important people who were descended from army officers. The third block of seats was reserved for wealthy merchants. Upper-class women were not allowed to sit with the men.

Stone seats were reserved for senators. The ordinary people sat on wooden benches.

# Keep your distance

The poorer people—men and women—were kept well away from the wealthy Romans. They sat on wooden benches high up in the arena. At the very top of the stadium were several rows of seats reserved for the wives of senators and other wealthy Romans. They were kept apart from the ordinary people by a high wall.

Gladiator fights were enjoyed so much that they were often illustrated in Roman mosaics, such as this.

Roman women of all classes loved to watch the gladiators fight. This piece of graffiti shows how women adored their glamorous fighting heroes:

*Celadus the gladiator, three times a winner, makes the girls swoon.*

Graffiti found at Pompeii, southern Italy, C. first century CE

# Roman society

In Roman times, the ruling classes lived a very different kind of life from the ordinary people. Wealthy Romans lived in beautiful houses in town. They often also had a country villa (a large, farming estate). Meanwhile, the ordinary Roman people lived in small cottages in the country or in crowded apartments in town.

11

# THE UPPER WALKWAY

Before taking your seat, make your way through the maze of ramps and passageways to the top of the stadium. From the upper walkway, you can enjoy a close-up view of the huge canvas awning, or *velarium*. The *velarium* is held in place by strong ropes attached to stone blocks on the ground outside the stadium. You might even see teams of Roman sailors operating the ropes.

**The upper walkway**

## Safety and comfort

Each section of seating had its own passageway leading to a different exit. It took less than 15 minutes for the Colosseum to be emptied as 50,000 people streamed out of 76 exits. Inside the stadium were marble troughs filled with drinking water, as well as public toilets. There were also many fountains sprinkling scented water to hide the stench of animals and blood.

These corridors would have been filled with thousands of spectators pouring into the amphitheater.

# Staging sea battles

Skilled Roman workmen used their shipbuilding skills to make the *velarium* and its masts. They also used these skills to build small-scale ships, which were used in the arena. There are records of spectacular sea battles being held in Roman amphitheaters. For these mock battles, the arena was flooded with several yards of water, and a crew of slaves acted out real battles that the Roman navy had fought. The battle lasted until the ships were broken up or sunk.

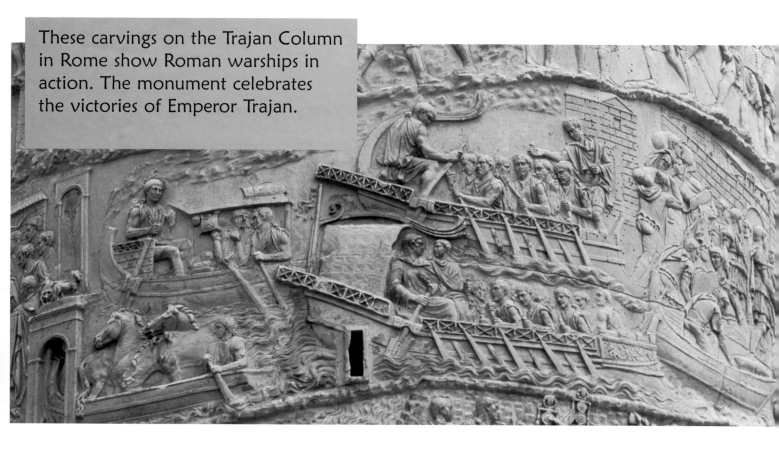

These carvings on the Trajan Column in Rome show Roman warships in action. The monument celebrates the victories of Emperor Trajan.

The historian Suetonius described a pretend sea battle, held in an amphitheater, which began with the performers chanting these words:

*Hail, Caesar! Those about to die salute you!*

Suetonius, *Lives of the Twelve Caesars*, second century CE

# Roman warships

The small-scale ships used in the arena were based on real Roman warships. These ships were long and narrow, each with a pointed, metal battering ram at the front. On the deck was a high tower where archers stood and fired burning arrows at their enemies. Some ships were also equipped with large wooden catapults that fired rocks and stones at enemy ships.

# THE EMPEROR'S BOX

While you're on your way to your seat, take a peek inside the emperor's box. This large area has lavishly painted walls and marble seating. It has plenty of room for the emperor and his guests, as well as for all his servants and slaves. The emperor's box is raised up high on a platform. This means that the emperor can be seen by everyone but still be close to the action.

**The emperor's box**

## Providing entertainment

Most emperors spent a fortune on building amphitheaters and putting on shows. The first Roman emperor, Augustus, put on shows involving a total of 10,000 gladiators. In 70 CE, Emperor Vespasian paid for the Colosseum to be built in Rome. Ten years later, it was opened by his son, Emperor Titus. To celebrate the opening, Titus put on 100 days of nonstop Games.

This 19th-century painting of Emperor Nero in his box shows him giving the "thumbs-down." This signaled that the gladiator must die.

# Emperor and judge

The emperor played a key role in the Games. He led the opening ceremony and presented the prizes. He also had to make some life-and-death decisions. Many gladiator fights ended with the defeated gladiator appealing to the crowd for mercy. The spectators then made a sign with their thumbs, which indicated their decision. (No one knows exactly what this sign was.) When the crowd's decision was unclear, the emperor had the deciding vote: life or death.

Emperor Gaius, who ruled from 37 to 41 CE, delighted in the cruelty of the Games. Here the historian Cassius Dio describes an especially bloodthirsty day in the arena:

*Once, when there was a shortage of condemned criminals to be given to the wild beasts, Emperor Gaius gave orders that some of the mob standing near to the benches be seized and thrown to them.*

Cassius Dio, *Roman History*, third century CE

# Different views

Most emperors loved the Games. The emperors Caligula and Commodus even fought in the arena dressed as gladiators. But Emperor Marcus Aurelius thought the Games were very cruel and tried to turn gladiator fights into athletic contests instead. Many Christians also saw the Games as cruel, and as Christianity spread across the Roman Empire, this view became widespread. In 399 CE, Emperor Honorius declared that there would be no more gladiator fights. This decision marked the end of the grand shows held in Roman amphitheaters.

Emperor Commodus loved to perform in the arena. Here he is dressed in a lion headdress like the ancient hero Hercules.

15

# A RINGSIDE SEAT

If you want an excellent view of the Games, take a ringside seat beside the arena. From here you will see the shows close-up, but you will also be safe from harm. Your ringside seat is raised 6.7 feet (2 m) above the level of the arena. There's also a high marble wall between you and the arena to stop wild animals from climbing into the crowd.

**A ringside seat**

Spectators at the Games felt perfectly safe with the arena wall to protect them from harm.

## Safety first

The protective wall around the arena had wooden rollers along the top. These were covered with polished marble to prevent any animals from gripping the wall. A net fence was also put up around the arena when savage beasts, such as lions, tigers, and bears, performed. As a final safety measure, archers crouched in niches in the marble wall, ready to shoot any animal that tried to escape into the crowd.

# An action-filled day

The audience could expect a full day of entertainment—the games usually started at 9 a.m. and lasted until late in the afternoon. A day in the amphitheater began with three hours of events featuring wild animals. These events were known as the *venationes*, which means "hunts" in Latin. They included hunts but also shows of performing animals and fights to the death. At midday there were two hours of public executions. During these brutal killings, most educated Romans left the arena and went out to lunch. At 2 p.m. it was time for the highlight of the day—gladiator fights.

**VENATIONES: SEE PAGES 26–27**

Some educated Romans enjoyed the gladiator fights but hated the hunts and the public executions. Philosopher and lawyer Cicero wrote:

*What pleasure can a civilized man get out of seeing a weak human being torn to pieces by a powerful animal or a splendid animal pierced by a hunting spear?*

Cicero, *Letters*, first century BCE

# Winners and prizes

At the end of the day's entertainments, the emperor (or another official) presented the prizes to the victorious gladiators. Gladiators could win money, a golden bowl, or a crown. They were also given a branch from a palm tree as a symbol of their victory. The victors ran around the edge of the arena, waving their palm branches in the air.

This Roman coin shows a gladiator receiving the crown of victory from Emperor Nero.

# THE ARENA

From your ringside seat, you'll have a superb view of the arena. It's a large oval stage a little smaller than a football field. The arena floor is wooden and covered by a thick layer of sand. The purpose of the sand is to soak up all the blood spilled during the day. Sometimes the sand is even dyed bright red to disguise the blood! In your seat, you're in a perfect position to spot the different types of gladiators.

**The arena**

## Gladiator types

Altogether, there were 15 types of Roman gladiator, each wearing different types of armor. Some represented ancient enemies of Rome. The gladiators known as Samnites were based on warriors from southern Italy. Samnites fought with a small sword and carried a long, oblong shield. They wore a helmet with a large crest and had one arm protector and one leg shield (known as a greave).

This collection of armor was found in a gladiators' training school in Pompeii, southern Italy.

Another group of gladiators based on an ancient enemy were the Thracians. The Thracian or Thrax carried a small, square shield and fought with a short, curved sword. He wore high greaves, an arm protector, and a wide-brimmed helmet.

One of the most popular gladiators was the *retiarius*, or "netman." He fought with a net, a trident, and a dagger. The netman had no helmet, which made him much more mobile than his opponents. He often fought against the *murmillo*, who wore a helmet crowned with a fish. The *murmillo* had a large shield to defend himself, one arm protector, and one greave.

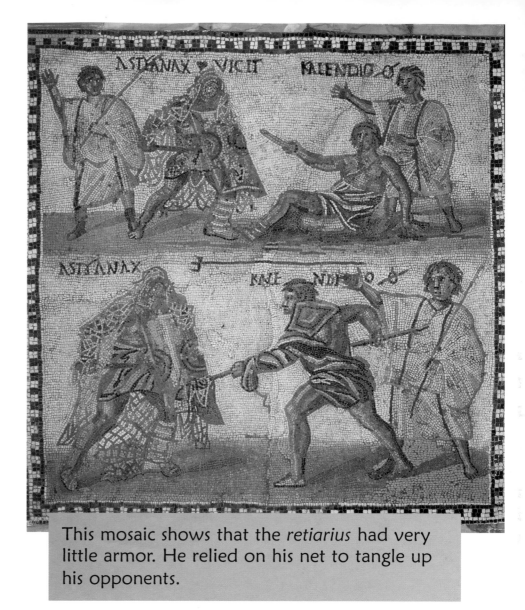

This mosaic shows that the *retiarius* had very little armor. He relied on his net to tangle up his opponents.

## Roman soldiers

Roman soldiers had similar armor and weapons to those of the gladiators, but the soldiers were much better protected. Roman foot soldiers (known as legionaries) wore short tunics and leather sandals studded with nails. They fought with daggers, swords, and javelins and carried large, rectangular shields. In battle, they wore iron helmets and their chests and shoulders were protected by metal breastplates.

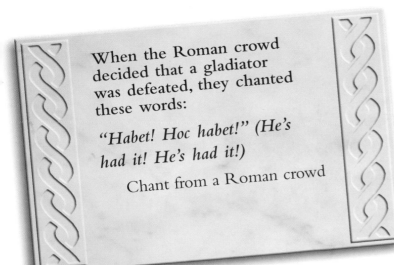

When the Roman crowd decided that a gladiator was defeated, they chanted these words:

*"Habet! Hoc habet!" (He's had it! He's had it!)*

Chant from a Roman crowd

GLADIATORS: SEE PAGE 9

# THE GATE OF DEATH

On either side of the arena, you can see two large gateways. At the start of the day, the gladiators enter the arena in a grand procession from the western gateway. Directly facing this entrance gate is the eastern gateway. It's known as the gate of death, because the bodies of the dead are carried through its archway.

**The gate of death**

## The ceremony of death

Whenever a gladiator was killed, attendants in the arena performed a special ritual. This involved figures dressed as Pluto, the god of death, and Mercury, the guide to the underworld. The dead gladiator was laid on a couch and taken by Mercury to the gate of death. During this solemn ceremony, musicians played mournful music on pipes, trumpets, and organs.

This painting shows the god Mercury, who was believed to guide the bodies of dead gladiators through the gate of death.

20

# Who were the gladiators?

Most gladiators were slaves or prisoners and were forced to fight in the arena. But some free men chose to give up their freedom and train as gladiators. Gladiators were paid a substantial sum when they joined up and each time they fought, so some men became gladiators to help them to pay their debts. Some were ex-soldiers who wished to test their skills, and some simply wanted to be heroes.

# Girls allowed

Sometimes, women fought in the arena. Emperor Nero liked to watch women fight, and Emperor Domitian held torchlit contests for female gladiators. But many Romans objected to women fighting, and in 200 CE Emperor Septimus Severus banned all female gladiators.

# Training and rewards

Gladiators were completely owned by their manager. They lived in special schools, where they trained very hard, learning fighting techniques. Life was tough, but the men were fed three good meals a day and were looked after by a doctor. A successful gladiator could win fame, glory, and prizes—and, importantly, his freedom. Gladiators only had to fight two or three times a year and after three to five years could be set free. However, few survived long enough.

Many Romans hated the sight of women fighting, but others loved to watch the female gladiators.

All new gladiators gave up their freedom and swore a solemn oath to their manager:

"*I will endure branding, chains, flogging, or death by the sword.*"

Petronius, Satiricon, first century CE

# A TRAPDOOR

In a quiet moment between the shows, try to take a closer look at one of the trapdoors that are scattered all over the arena. These hidden entrances are used to create some very dramatic surprises. You'll see that the door is fixed on hinges so it can be opened from below. A wooden ramp leads up to the trapdoor. This means that animals, such as tigers and lions, can be released into the arena. At intervals during the games, a trapdoor may suddenly open, as a fighter or animal makes an unexpected entrance!

**A trapdoor**

## A terrible death

Trapdoors were often used in the midday events when prisoners were put to death. Groups of prisoners were led into the arena, where they waited in horror. Then, without any warning, the trapdoors would open, and out would spring lions and tigers to tear them to pieces. In the later years of the empire, many people complained about this bloodthirsty method of execution.

Emperor Titus ruled from 39 to 81 CE. He loved the excitement and drama of the Games.

# Plays in the arena

Sometimes, trapdoors were used for special effects in plays. These plays told a story, using scenery and costumes, but they were really excuses to kill people. Actors in the arena usually acted out a Roman legend. One popular subject was the legend of Dirce, who was tied to a bull. Dirce was played by a female prisoner, and the play always ended with her death.

# Roman theaters

Many Romans preferred to watch plays in theaters, rather than amphitheaters. Roman theaters were large open-air structures built on the sides of hills. These stone theaters formed a semicircle, with rows of tiered seats rising from the stage. Educated Romans enjoyed tragedies, based on the dramas of the ancient Greeks, but the ordinary people preferred to watch comedies and mimes.

The organizers of the Games loved to surprise the crowd with unexpected special effects. Here historian Cassius Dio describes how Emperor Titus added a few surprises of his own.

*He threw down into the stadium little wooden balls with inscriptions, one promising food, another clothing, another horses, cattle, or slaves. Those who seized the balls could claim their prize.*

Cassius Dio, *Roman History*, third century CE

The play of Orpheus and the animals was often acted out in the arena, but it always ended with Orpheus being mauled to death.

23

# AN ELEVATOR

Your tour of a Roman amphitheater isn't complete until you've explored beneath the arena floor. To reach this underground area, you can take an elevator, but don't expect anything stylish. This is the lift used to take the animals up to the arena. It consists of a cage fixed to some very strong ropes. The ropes are attached to a set of winches, and slaves tug on the ropes to make the lift go up and down.

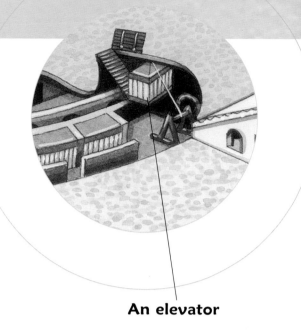

**An elevator**

## Going underground

As the lift descended below the arena, a very different world began. Here it was dark, noisy, and smelly. Narrow corridors led off in all directions, and there were many people hurrying around. The corridors would have echoed with the sounds of animals roaring, officials shouting orders, and the prisoners moaning.

PRISONERS: SEE PAGES 28-29

Elevators carried the animals up to the arena. They emerged through trapdoors or through gates at the side of the stage.

# Running the Games

By the first century CE, there were more than 90 Games a year. Organizers had to provide a constant supply of animals and people to be killed in the arena. Hundreds of slaves and prisoners worked night and day helping to set up the shows and clearing up the mess afterward. The hardest jobs were done by the animal keepers, known as *bestiarii*. They cared for the animals and led them into the arena. They also had to perform, fighting unarmed against savage beasts.

ANIMALS: SEE PAGES 26–27

Clearing up the arena was a major task, especially after the slaughter of the public executions.

It was hard to supply enough animals for all the events in the arena. In this letter from Turkey, Cicero explains why he has not sent more panthers for the Games.

*The problem is there is a remarkable shortage of the animals. . . . Nevertheless, your request is being taken care of and as many panthers as are available will be yours.*

Cicero, *Letters*, first century BCE

## Roman slaves

There were millions of slaves in the Roman Empire. Some of them had been captured and sold into slavery, while many others were born into a slave family. Some slaves had to work in the amphitheater or as miners or builders, but others had an easier life. Roman slaves worked on the land and in homes, shops, and workshops. Some educated slaves worked as doctors, librarians, or teachers or helped to run the empire.

# CAGES FOR ANIMALS

Once your eyes have gotten used to the dark, follow the sounds of roaring, screeching, and bellowing to the animals' cages. To reach the cages, you'll have to walk through a maze of narrow corridors. The corridors are made deliberately narrow so that the animals can't turn around and bite their keepers.

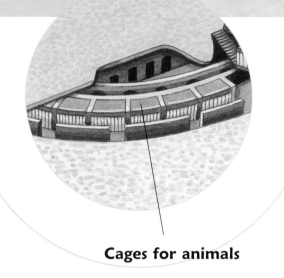

**Cages for animals**

## Wild beasts from afar

Housed in tiny cages were animals from all over the Roman Empire. Lions, leopards, crocodiles, bulls, ostriches, hippos, and bears were all crowded together. They had been brought from distant lands such as Egypt, Morocco, and Syria.

This is the underground lion pit of an arena in Tunisia, North Africa. It has unusually wide corridors.

## Animal empire

The amazing animal shows in the arena were not just intended to amuse the crowd. They were also meant to impress the Roman people with the size and variety of their empire. The Roman Empire reached its largest size in 117 CE. At that time, the empire stretched from Britain in the north to northern Africa in the south and reached as far east as present-day Iraq.

# Hunting and fighting

Animal shows (known as *venationes*) always opened with wild animals such as deer, bears, or even elephants being tracked down by skilled hunters. Then came the fights between trained fighters (known as *venatores*) and the animals. The *venatores* fought savagely against lions, bulls, and elephants, weaving and dodging to amuse the crowd. Other entertainment included violent fights between two wild beasts, such as lions against tigers or bulls against bears.

Sometimes the crowd showed pity for the animals. Here Cicero describes a surprising reaction to a special show:

*The last day was for the elephants. The crowd showed much astonishment, but no enjoyment. There was even a feeling of pity, a sense that the monsters had something human about them.*

Cicero, *Letters*, first century BCE

This engraved dish shows Roman hunters chasing a leopard and some antelopes.

## The show must go on

The *venationes* usually ended with a show of trained animals performing tricks. Bears would dance or elephants would sit up and beg. Some creatures didn't perform any tricks but were displayed because they were so rare. When Emperor Julius Caesar first showed a giraffe in Rome, in 46 BCE, everyone in the crowd was astonished!

27

# CELLS FOR PRISONERS

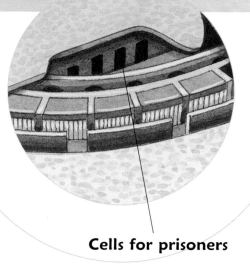

Close to the animals' cages, you will see some small, brick rooms. In these prison cells, all kinds of criminals are crowded together, waiting to go to their death in the arena. You may also hear some Christian prisoners singing hymns. Christians were condemned to death in the arena because they refused to worship the Roman gods, but they often kept up their spirits by singing.

**Cells for prisoners**

## Public executions

Prisoners were executed in the arena in many horrible ways. They could be burned at the stake, crucified on wooden crosses, or mauled to death by wild animals. Sometimes two prisoners, armed only with swords, had to fight each other to the death. As soon as the fight was over, the winner had to fight a new opponent and kept on going until he was killed. The final survivor was usually finished off by a wild beast.

Many prisoners had to fight for their lives against wild beasts. Often they had no weapons at all.

# Crime and punishment

The Romans set up strict laws, and anyone accused of breaking these laws was put on trial. A judge ran the trial, and a group of local citizens—known as the jury—decided if the accused was innocent or guilty. Lawbreakers could be sent to work in the mines, forced to work as gladiators, or put to death in the arena. Wealthy Romans were punished less severely than the poor—they were usually fined or banished to distant parts of the Empire. Many Romans believed that public executions provided a powerful warning not to break the law, though others complained that they were cruel.

Roman lawbreakers were often forced to do hard labor. This carving shows three prisoners roped together.

Like many educated Romans, Seneca hated the public executions and found them bloodthirsty and cruel.

*I happened to arrive [in the arena] at the time of the lunch-hour interlude, expecting some light and witty entertainment . . . a rest from human blood. Far from it. What I saw was murder, pure and simple.*

Seneca, *Letters*, first century BCE

# Persecuting Christians

By the third century CE, there were Christians in many parts of the Roman Empire. The emperors saw the Christians as a threat to their power because they refused to worship the Roman gods, and thousands of Christians were put to death in amphitheaters. This cruel persecution finally came to an end at the start of the fourth century. In 313 CE, Emperor Constantine declared that Christians were allowed to follow their own religion.

# TIMELINE

**BCE**

**c.750**    The Latin people found the city of Rome.

**c.100**    The Romans start to build wooden stadiums.

**46**    Emperor Julius Caesar holds animal shows in Rome. One of the animals on display is a giraffe.

**27**    Augustus becomes the first emperor. During his reign, he holds Games to entertain the Roman people.

**CE**

**43**    The Romans conquer Britain.

**64**    Emperor Nero starts persecuting Christians. Nero also encourages female gladiator fights.

**72**    Emperor Vespasian gives orders for the Colosseum to be built in Rome.

**80**    The Colosseum is opened by Emperor Titus with 100 days of nonstop Games.

**c.100**    The Romans start to build stone stadiums all over the empire.

**117**    The Roman Empire reaches its largest size, under Emperor Hadrian.

**161**    Marcus Aurelius becomes emperor and rules for the next 19 years. He tries to turn the gladiator fights into athletics contests with no bloodshed.

**180**    Commodus becomes emperor. During his 12-year reign, he makes many appearances in the arena of the Colosseum.

**200**    Emperor Septimus Severus bans female gladiators.

**303**    Emperor Diocletian leads a savage campaign to persecute Christians.

**313**    Emperor Constantine announces that Christians in the empire may worship freely.

**399**    Emperor Honorius bans gladiator fights, marking the end of the public Games.

**476**    The Roman Empire collapscs.

# GLOSSARY

**anonymous** Unknown or not known.

**arena** The central area of a stadium, where all the events take place.

**attendant** A helper.

*bestiarii* Keepers of the wild animals that performed in shows in the arena. The *bestiarii* often also fought against the animals in the arena.

**breastplate** A fitted metal chest plate that is worn by soldiers and some gladiators.

**emperor** The head of the Roman Empire.

*equites* A class of important people in Roman society who were descended from army officers.

**execution** The act of putting someone to death as a punishment for a crime.

**Games** The entertainments provided for the public in Roman amphitheaters.

**gladiator** Someone who has been trained to fight in an amphitheater as a public entertainment.

**greaves** Fitted metal plates that soldiers and some gladiators wore on their lower legs.

**legionaries** Foot soldiers in the Roman army.

*murmillo* A gladiator who fought with a dagger and wore a helmet that looked like a fish.

**netman** A gladiator who fights with a net and trident. "Netman" is the English name for *retiarius*.

**persecution** Unfair treatment or punishment.

**quarry** A place where stone is dug out of the ground.

*retiarius* A gladiator who fights with a net and trident.

**ritual** A set of actions that are always performed in the same way as part of a ceremony.

**Samnite** A gladiator who fights with a small sword and carries a long, oblong shield.

**senator** One of a group of men, known as the senate, who help to govern Rome.

**story** A floor or layer in a building.

**Thracian** A gladiator who fights with a short, curved sword and carries a small, square shield. Another name for a Thracian is a Thrax.

**trident** A long-handled fork with three sharp prongs, used as a weapon.

**underworld** The place where the Romans believed that people went when they died.

*velarium* Canvas awning that covered part of the amphitheater and gave the crowd some shade from the midday sun.

*venationes* Events in the arena involving animals.

**warrior** Man who fights battles.

**winch** A lifting machine made by a rope wound over a drum.

# FURTHER INFORMATION

## Books

Whittock, Martyn. *The Colosseum and the Roman Forum.* Heinemann Library, 2002.

Chandler, Fiona, Sam Taplin, and Jane Bingham. *The Roman World.* Usborne, 2001.

Solway, Andrew and Stephen Biesty. *Rome.* Oxford University Press, 2003.

## Websites

depthome.brooklyn.cuny.edu/classics/
gladiatr/index.htm
A large, well-illustrated site on the Roman Games, including sections on the amphitheater, gladiators and animal events (*venatio*).

www.vroma.org/%7Ebmcmanus/
arena.html
A history of the Colosseum, a guide to different types of gladiators, and a description of events held at the Colosseum.

www.pbs.org/wnet/warriorchallenge/
gladiators/profile.html
An illustrated guide to types of gladiators, with good information on their armor, weapons, and fighting methods.

catholic-resources.org/AncientRome/
Colisseum.htm
Twelve excellent photos of the Colosseum in Rome.

www.bbc.co.uk/history/ancient/romans/
launch_gms_gladiator.shtml
An interactive game, in which you take the part of a gladiator and can even dress him for battle.

www.roman-empire.net/
A very large site on Roman history and culture. Includes a children's section.

www.bbc.co.uk/schools/romans/
A lively website on the Romans, organized by topics. It includes activities and fun facts.

# INDEX

Page numbers in **bold** refer to illustrations.